WINK

WINK

A LIFE STORY

EDDIE A. WINKLEY

gatekeeper press™
Columbus, Ohio

Wink: A Life Story

Published by Gatekeeper Press

2167 Stringtown Rd, Suite 109

Columbus, OH 43123-2989

www.GatekeeperPress.com

Library of Congress Control Number: 2020944383

ISBN (hardcover): 9781662903892

ISBN (paperback): 9781662903908

eISBN: 9781662903915

In loving memory of Grandmother Goldie Rimpson

"We all expect to achieve great things, but you must be committed to hard work, your faith, and education to obtain all the precious gifts this life has in store for you." - Eddie A. Winkley

All proceeds of this book will go towards educational and community outreach activities.

To every young person that reads this book,
the world needs your;

Wisdom to make good decisions.

Imagination to accomplish things that the world hasn't seen before.

Nobleness to make the world a better place.

Kindness to bring joy to the lives of others.

Author Bio:

Eddie A. Winkley is a retired Supervisory Special Agent with the Federal Bureau of Investigation (FBI). He is a first-time author who wrote this book as one of his bucket list items. Eddie grew up in the inner city of Kansas City, Mo., where he attended Southwest High School. He furthered his education at Lincoln University (Mo.) where he obtained a Bachelor of Science in Criminal Justice. He later attended Webster University and received a Master of Arts in Management. He presently lives in Maryland with his wife. He enjoys mentoring youth and participating in community outreach activities.

IN AUTUMN, WHEN THE FARMERS STARTED TO GATHER VEGGIES AND FRUIT, A BABY BOY WAS BORN BY THE NAME OF WINK, WHO HIS MOTHER THOUGHT WAS EXTREMELY CUTE.

AS THE LEAVES STARTED TO CHANGE
THEIR COLORS AND FALL, WINK BEGAN
TO ESCAPE HIS CRADLE AND CRAWL.

WINK WAS IN NO HURRY TO TAKE HIS
FIRST STEP TO WALK; HE WAS SLOW TO
UTTER HIS FIRST WORD TO TALK.

WINK WAS NOT SHY...HE JUST HAD
NOTHING TO SAY. HE WANTED TO
SPEND ALL DAY LONG AT PLAY.

HIS MOTHER DECIDED TO HAVE ONLY ONE CHILD
BECAUSE WINK WAS SO ACTIVE AND WILD.

ONCE HE FINALLY LEARNED TO WALK
AND TALK, WINK WAS STRONG AND
HAD WISDOM LIKE A HAWK.

WHEN IT WAS TIME FOR WINK TO
START SCHOOL, HE WAS SCARED
BUT WANTED TO APPEAR COOL.

HE TRIED TO FIT IN BY BEING FUNNY TO
MAKE FRIENDS; HE DRESSED FANCY TO
KEEP UP WITH THE LATEST TRENDS.

SOME KIDS IN MIDDLE SCHOOL WERE MEAN
AND CRUEL, BUT WINK WANTED NO TROUBLE
AND JUST HUNG HIS HEAD LIKE A MULE.

WINK PLAYED IN MIDDLE SCHOOL AND WANTED
TO BE THE CLASS CLOWN. HIS GRADES
SUFFERED, MAKING HIS MOTHER FROWN.

HIS MOTHER SCOLDED HIM AND TOLD
HIM TO BEHAVE; IF NOT, HE WOULD BE
FORCED TO LIVE WITH BEARS IN A CAVE.

WINK TOOK HER ADVICE AND STARTED
TO ACT GOOD. HE BEHAVED WELL
AS HE KNEW HE COULD.

WINK USED HIS ENERGY TO PLAY MANY
SPORTS, SPENDING HIS TIME ON BASEBALL
FIELDS AND BASKETBALL COURTS.

WINK ALSO PLAYED FOOTBALL ON A
WINNING TEAM, WHICH HELPED HIM STAY
FOCUSED AND BUILD SELF-ESTEEM.

WINK'S RELIGIOUS FAITH BECAME
STRONG. IT KEPT HIM OUT OF TROUBLE
WHEN HE WANTED TO DO WRONG.

WHEN WINK GREW UP INTO HIS TEENAGE YEARS, HE NOTICED BUMPS ON HIS FACE WHICH BROUGHT HIM TO TEARS.

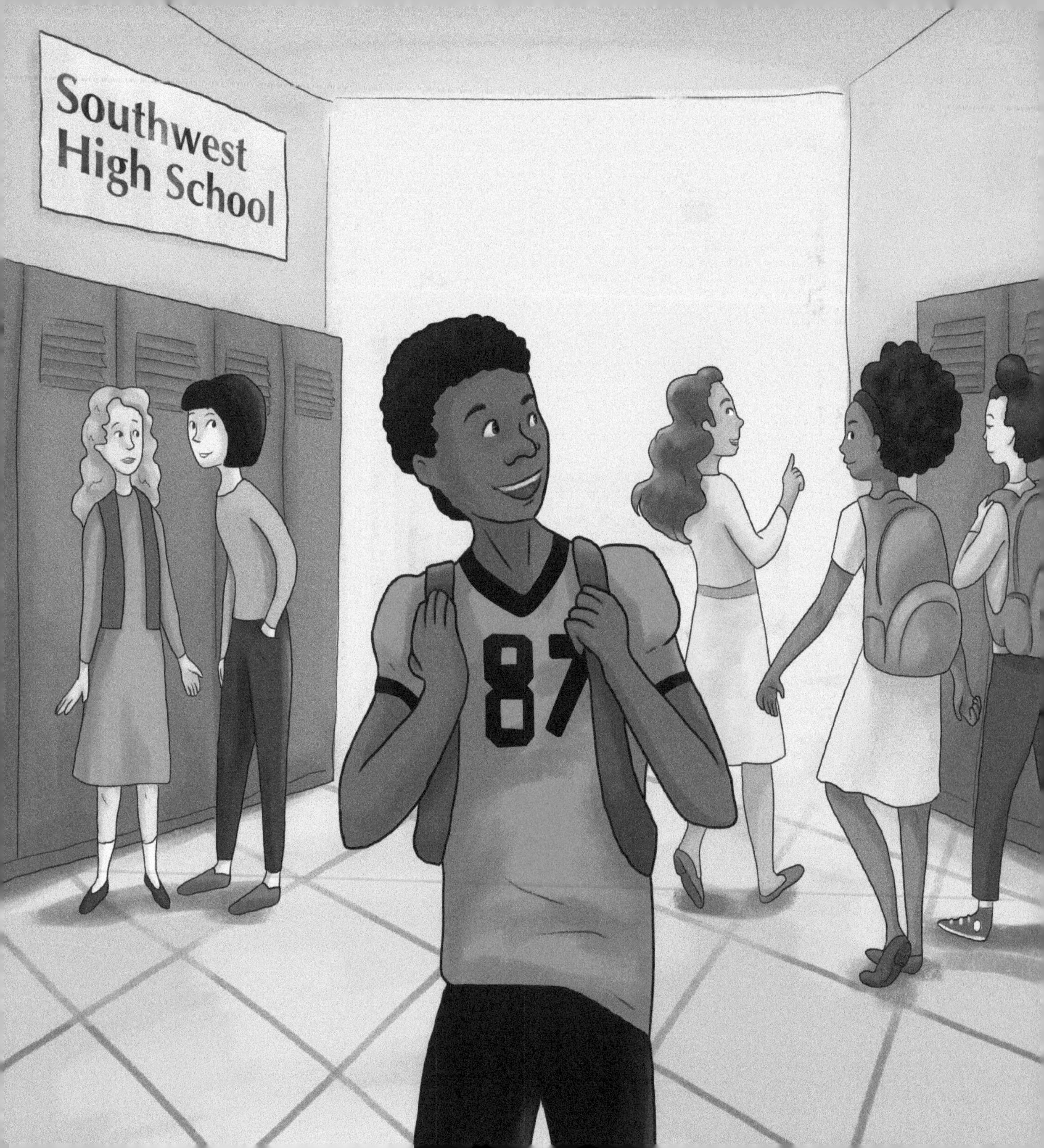
Southwest
High School
87

HE ENTERED HIGH SCHOOL AND TRIED TO
KEEP TO HIMSELF, UNTIL HE NOTICED GIRLS,
WHICH MADE HIM HAPPY AS AN ELF.

HIS MOTHER PUSHED HIM TO STUDY
HARD, PRAYING THAT HE WOULD
RECEIVE A GOOD REPORT CARD.

SHE WANTED WINK TO BE SMART AND
GET AN EDUCATION, SO HE COULD BE A
GOOD CITIZEN IN THIS GREAT NATION.

WINK RECEIVED A DIPLOMA WHICH WAS
GREAT, AND THEN HE DECIDED TO GO TO
COLLEGE WITH HIS FOOTBALL TEAMMATE.

WHEN WINK WENT TO COLLEGE, HE
WAS DELIGHTED. ALL HIS FAMILY AND
FRIENDS WERE SO EXCITED.

THEY TOLD HIM IF HE STUDIED HARD HE
WOULD DO VERY WELL. WINK WANTED HIS
DEGREE THEREFORF HE WOULD NOT FAIL.